The
Perfect
Garden

by Sarah Weeks
✳
illustrated by
Janet Montecalvo

MODERN CURRICULUM PRESS
Pearson Learning Group

The air was warm. A soft breeze blew through the forest. It was the sweet smell of spring. Birds were busy building their nests. Squirrels jumped from branch to branch chattering happily. At the edge of the woods a large gray rabbit lifted his head. He closed his eyes and breathed deeply.

Perry opened his eyes. Then he slowly let out his breath.

"There is nothing in the world that smells as sweet as a newly planted garden." Perry knew all about gardens. Last spring and summer he had visited the Conners' garden almost every day. He knew about tender carrots and young lettuce. He knew about radishes so new they were still white and not yet hot.

The Conners lived near the edge of the forest
in a large white house. There was a big porch that
went all the way around the back. On hot days,
Perry would enjoy a nap in the cool dirt under the
porch. When evening came, the Conners would
have their supper outside. Then Perry would roam
over to the garden for his own evening meal.

Mr. and Mrs. Conner lived in the house with their dog, Bob. He was a large spotted hound. Bob had a scary face and fierce, sharp teeth. He also had the harshest bark.

Every spring, Mr. Conner took his shovel, his rake, and his hoe out to his garden. Then he and Mrs. Conner would decide which vegetables should go where.

"Peas over here! Lettuce over there! Beans along the back!" Mrs. Conner would say. Perry would roam around and watch. They watered the garden and pulled out weeds. Perry could tell that they loved the garden. He was glad. He loved it too!

As Perry sat at the edge of the forest, he heard the harshest sound he had ever heard. It was not the squeak of the swings in the Cliffords' backyard. It was not the friendly hum of Mr. Richard's lawn mower. This was the harshest sound Perry could imagine. It seemed to come from the Conners' garden. Perry hopped to the edge of the yard to take a look.

Perry hid under a bush. He had a good view of
the garden. What he saw made no sense at all!
Instead of the usual tools, Mr. Conner had a pile
of long sticks. He also had a large roll of something
else. What were they doing to the garden?

"This will keep that pest away," Mr. Conner said as he pounded a stick into the ground. "I will not spend another summer letting my work get nibbled down to nothing."

"Only we will eat the lettuce this year," said Mrs. Conner. Then she tested the pole to see if it was steady.

"I respect wildlife," said Mr. Conner. "Unless it eats my carrots."

"What are they talking about?" wondered Perry. Why were they pounding in the sticks? Perry roamed around the garden. As he watched, Mr. and Mrs. Conner pounded in sticks all the way around the garden. Then they hooked some wire to the sticks. It looked strange.

"There," said Mr. Conner. "Nothing will get through this."

"Good job!" said Mrs. Conner.

The Conners and Bob walked back to the house. Perry hopped over to the garden for a closer look.

In a flash, Perry dug a hole under the new fence. Then he squeezed through it. Next he ate a new lettuce leaf. Just as he chewed off another bite he heard a fierce growl. Suddenly he came face to face with Bob. Perry couldn't move. His ears stood straight up. His nose didn't dare wiggle.

Bob started to howl. It was a horrible, fierce noise. The Conners ran out to the garden to see what was the matter.

"I can't believe it!" shouted Mr. Conner. "Something is eating my vegetables again!"

Bob kept howling until Mrs. Conner sent him back to the house. Perry squeezed back under the fence and headed home.

Perry was safe in his cozy hole. He thought
about everything that had happened that day.

"Humans are so strange," he thought. "First
they plant a lovely garden. Then they put that
ugly thing around it. Why would they do that?"
Then, suddenly, he understood. "They did it for
me! Now Bob can't bother me while I'm eating."

Perry went to sleep thinking about Mr. and Mrs. Conner. He couldn't believe they had gone to all of that trouble—just so he could visit the garden without worrying about Bob. How could he thank the Conners for their kindness?

Perry finally figured it out. If the Conners were fond of having rabbits in their garden, then he would invite every rabbit he knew to visit it. He felt a bit sorry for Bob. But most of all, Perry felt lucky to have friends who would make a perfect garden for him.